C000015490

# Stance

# Stance

## MARK BRAYLEY

Patrician Press ● Manningtree

# Contents

First published by Patrician Press in a paperback edition 2016
For more information: www.patricianpress.com

First published as a paperback edition by Patrician Press 2016

E-book edition published by Patrician Press 2016

Copyright © Mark Brayley 2016

The right of Mark Brayley to be identified as the author of this work has been asserted in accordance with the Copyright, Designs and Patents Act of 1988.

All rights reserved. No part of this document may be reproduced or transmitted in any form or by any means, electronic, mechanical, photocopying, recording, or otherwise, without prior written permission of Patrician Press.

British Library Cataloguing in Publication Data. A catalogue record for this book is available from the British Library.

ISBN paperback edition 978-0-9934945-9-8

ISBN e-book edition 978-0-9934945-8-1

Printed and bound in Peterborough by Printondemand-worldwide

# Introduction

This book of poems is a collection of lipograms and, as such, they omit the letter i. The letter i is the fourth most used letter in the English language and without it there can be no –ing; there can be no is; there can be no infinity, no intrinsic indignity, nor any implicit nihilism. Most importantly there can be no personal pronoun, I.

This forces the poetry into a more objective stance, and away from the poetic pitfalls of solipsism and narcissism. With the ego almost expunged, characters can carry the language, objects can be observed, and the past is brought to the fore.

Furthermore, writing with the constraint of the lipogram bars particular words and phrases; the linguistically dexterous search for alternatives often delivering something more effective and interesting than what was first conceived.

Not content with the lipogram of i, the collection begins with a lipogram of e, i, o and u to form a univocalic (using only one vowel) in the poem Madam La La's and also includes a lipogram of i and u in the poem Zoetrope.

# Madam La La's

Madam La La's all-star gay drag act

at camp Manhattan salsa bar –

all brawn and bras and cha-cha-chas;

a fast track gala *à la*

class acts, sarcasm and schnapps,

back, crack and sack wax,

spray tan and bad Wall-Mart mascara.

Wham-bam! Thanks, mam!

Man, what larks?

Crank and PCP,

glad rags and handbags at dawn,

half can-can; half walk.

A grand sashay saga

as all standard snatch scrams.

Alas! Drama at Manhattan Parkway:

Fag hags fall and flash gash at lads.

Brass tacks, brats;

Gaydar says, away!

Fag hags hang back.

Lads gag at haggard slags

and start a fatal fray.

Bad karma!

Madam La La calls a cab

and slams a charm at ham glam fag hag shams.

All-star gay drag act at camp Manhattan salsa bar –

all brawn and bras and cha-cha-chas.

# All the Scraps of Paper Are Here

All the scraps of paper are here,

heaped up;

the scrawled on envelopes

of the letters from lawyers and banks

that meant less than words.


Those scraps that have escaped

seek refuge as bookmarks

to be uncovered decades hence.

Those books, others shoulders

for me to stand on, now

loom from shelves –

sonnets and cantos,

cherubs upon zephyrs,

nymphs and dryads –

to steer my pen.


A lazy Dylan LP on the record player

and there's me,

surrounded by tomes

of unmade verse.


An equal measure of doodles

stack up from when words were absent

but today

the chores are left undone,

plates unstacked and beds unchanged,

and loops and curves of letters

take precedent.

# Between Atoms and
# Empty Space

Between atoms and empty space

you spoke.

Your words hazed at me, too far away

to count.

Trapped by blankets

and aloof to each other, we made love.

The smallest of deaths traced the letter o

above your mouth,

before we fell

to slumber.

Then

the command post of your words

spelt out how we would be.

Apart;

separated by dates and oceans,

by whens and wheres.

A show here, a party there;

March and May;

New York and Amsterdam;

the dream.

Our dream.


Remember when dates

were the soft flames of hope

that brought us together?

# Summer Clothes

You take your summer clothes,

vacuum sealed packages,

from the loft

and unwrap three seasons past.


You shake out the uselessness

and the creases,

and as you do

the breeze releases

the breath of blossom;

of London's musk;

of Hyde Park peddle boats

and Soho's dusk.

You hold them up:

short shorts and cropped tops;

the sarong that made us

laugh;

the blouse you wore

when the days stayed longer;

gossamer petals that lay

smooth and tender over your back

or wrapped around your slender flank.

That dress

and the moment

that we touched.

They hang on you well

just as your lover

hangs on your word,

ready to dress you

once more.

# Play

Go out and pound the ground

around the chalk squares

of your hopscotch course.

Learn the balance of power

between two or three

or four or more.

Race. To run and scream

does not make you feral.

Play tag. Play jokes.

Play dead, you gruesome brutes.

Yes, even face the end of play

as a game

you'll never master.

Scamper up boughs and branches

of trees worn smooth by those who've gone before.

Use the edge of your sneaker

to push down the nettles and the ferns

to construct dens or even forts.

You'll need to know the use of walls

when you're an adult.

Become a general and marshal your forces

for the day when you shall lead

or be led.


Use bamboo canes to slay the demons

that haunt your dreams.

Fall off your scooter and run home,

blood on your elbows, palms or knees,

to learn that mother really cares.

Leave the shackles of that controller,

locked by the thumbs;

or the albatross laptop around your neck

that only tells you that you're not

good enough.


Strangers are not all dangerous, most

just walk on by. Those who do stop,

are probably just rapped at the wry memory

of the days when they were free.

# The Paragons of
# Bertrand Russell

Turn the page.

No. Stop.

Go back to what he says

about God and how

the myth falls apart

because He would never have

created a brood so flawed,

and therefore cannot be.

That's us –

work, eat, sleep, buy,

work, eat, sleep, buy,

work, eat, sleep, bye –

the flawed ones.

That's how he saw us

and perhaps why He has turned away

or been turned away.

Once, we were paragons,

even the most evolved,

and yet

as fatally flawed

as any hero.


Now look.

# FR 4173

Seatbelts fastened,

somewhere below people are under clouds

as we make the dozy afternoon return

to England.

The steward has the last word

of the other language

left at Bergamo,

as he attempts to sell duty free

perfume and booze.

Not a drop of laudanum.

At the quadruple panes

we attempt to harness the heat

of bare heaven,

to covet the warmth of lost sun

before we return

to jumpers and boots.


What would Shelley have made

of the sunbeam-proof clouds from here,

over earth and ocean,

beyond proof?

What rapture of the towers,

above the showers and the shade

of noonday dreams?


Dollops of gelato

across the curve of the earth,

a flotsam sea,

and then the stratosphere

where endless darkness speaks.

We snap photos of snow capped peaks,

below, and the Alps beckon for another story

as yet untold.

Once, a hero rowed across the lake,

below, fuelled by brandy,

to escape the war;

and once,

below, a monster was born;

and Goethe saw youth blend to grey today,

as we sat, seatbelts fastened,

above,

at twenty-seven thousand feet.

# Safe from Home

The general's daughter sat

at the desk and declared,

"More!"

More of what,

she could not say.

Her mother tongue was torn

apart by her father's trade.

She completed course after

course after course

on the campus

but was never known

for how she related

to the war.

Her homeland shuddered

under her father's hand

but she was sheltered

under the safety of the general's money

and the books they bought,

course after course.

Thus protected,

a tower for refuge,

she never really learnt

but always demanded

more.

# Ocean Bound Hope

## Ocean Bound Hope 1

Ocean bound hope sank beneath a news reel

we consumed amongst the others

you were lost to your mother before you lost her

all was calm at the outset

the money was settled a bond made

stronger than the coarse rope that held the boat

to the dock to suffer no more

ocean bound hope

sank and all souls were lost

there'll be another news reel another

hundred or three

more days that pass the same

when people drown for freedom

that's sold as coca cola splashes

on the proud coffers of the empty banks

and you queue to pay

through the nose for the chance to drown

## Ocean Bound Hope 2

Ocean bound hope

sank beneath a news reel we consumed

amongst the others you were lost to your mother

before you lost her all was calm

at the outset the money was settled

a bond made stronger

than the coarse rope

that held the boat to the dock to suffer

no more ocean bound

hope sank and all souls were lost

there'll be another

news reel another

hundred or three more days that pass

the same when people drown

for freedom that's sold

as coca cola splashes on the proud

coffers of the empty banks and you queue

to pay through the nose

for the chance to drown

## Ocean Bound Hope 3

Ocean bound

hope sank beneath

a news reel we consumed

amongst the others you

were lost

to your mother before you

lost her all

was calm at the outset

the money was

settled a bond

made stronger than the coarse rope that held

the boat to the dock

to suffer no more

ocean bound

hope sank

and all souls were lost there'll be another

news

reel

another hundred

or three more days that pass

the same when people drown for freedom

that's sold

as coca cola splashes

on the proud coffers

of the empty banks and you

queue to pay through the nose for the chance

to drown

# Zoetrope

There's not one place we went

that now welcomes me alone.

Each space rejects my memory

of loss and shows less care

than anyone else dares reveal,

as *My Other* fades beyond

what was once the sky.

We posed for photos here.

Who knows where they are now.

A gentle breeze swells the hope

that we can be once more.

Salt, seaweed and blasted sand.

Sharp tears attack the eyes and

the man, the dejected reject man,

flees the scene to go home

alone and feast on spleen.

TV Package meals fall short

of stop gap love. No comfort

food here. Only stewed regret.

The remote control has never felt

so remote as now. And show

on show, on show, the same.

Repeat. Repeat. Repeat.

My head – a zoetrope of all we had,

as we stepped

from chance to chance

towards

the end.

# Burn

Burn

a candle from one end

to the other,

not both at once.

# The Farouche

# Farceur

The farce, the latest West End smash,

wasn't about the loss of well pressed trousers

or even a case of star-crossed luggage.

The theme of the play

was the penchant for pederasty

that should have been extraneous to pedagogy

but wasn't.

From hurt to head

and head to heart

to pen to page

to rehearsal room to dress rehearsal

and here

to performance,

not a drop of the real was lost,

only added to.

Stage left, cassock adorned satyrs

use the naked flesh of boys as hassocks.

The set, bedecked as an orgy

of sarcenet and sandalwood,

formed a red den

of a smoke hazed fantasy

school room,

 resplendent as a poppy husk.

*The truth was far more grey.*

*Rather than carved dragons,*

*there were photos of teaboys*

*from yesteryear;*

*the eyes portrayed a cherub's lament.*

All the other archetypal characters,

through three acts,

heaven, purgatory and hell,

form a mad cap mockery of the scene,

unaware of what has been,

but

the lead role was school master as aesthete,

aesthete as school master –

the master aesthete.

The actor who took on the role was a star,

stellar-born to act.

There was an obscene charm

that made all else gauche.

Dappled on a shallowness.

All who saw the play could only be rapt

by the suave lullaby of decadence offered,

and henceforth crash to the floor at the dénouement

and the comeuppance due.

*Only, deeper,*

*he wasn't suave.*

*He taught maths and fondled.*

*The hand, a fomenter on the knee,*

*snatched away*

*at the dénouement of a footfall*

*or a knock at the door.*

Between tragedy and comedy

the farouche farceur felt

that perhaps the great Greek

scholars had been wrong.

The farce he'd made had not

the force to purge the human soul.

# The Man from Uncle

As avuncular as dust on nettles,

you open-handedly taught us

the power of the slap.

You came at me once,

your clenched hams ready

to teach me a lesson.


You're no blood to us,

just lust

stolen from a decade of shame.

We used to say

we would love you

to fuck off.


But now,

as we are grown –

our maps cover more pages –

and you are grown weaker

by the day,

your dull set tones grumble

your lack of content.

You've softened

and we can separate

the man from uncle.

# Turtle

You were solvent vapours,

a wake waft of punk.

You won't remember

when those two French students,

agog at your green mohawk,

came to the graveyard to buy hash.

You wrapped the wrapper

of your Marlboro packet

around a stone

and told me to keep my flapper shut.

The fraud complete,

you laughed

at the curses

they threw at us

and spent the ten pound note

on glue.

# The Judgemental Doctor

You vent

spleen but offer

no rhyme

nor reason

for the substance

of your bubble

of the learned

man.

Come back

ten years from now

when you have butchered

your holy cow

and the horror,

the horror's

etched

across your face.

Scream

for the want of cannon's mouth

and know that you have burst.

Replace your shattered core

and look around

and learn the value

of what you've found.

# M.A.D

From oath to sworn testament;

from covenant to charter;

out of every truth;

every bond ever made;

out of all that could be

mutually assured;

we found our way to that.

# Cups

Your coffee cups adorn the space

on the ledge below the pane –

glazed calm, two-tone brown –

as the world beyond churns

through another day.

They form a rank of perfect symmetry

to counteract the chaos of cars

and busses and commuters' feet.

The central cup reflects a beam

from somewhere further back.

They yearn for an orange tablecloth

from the decade of flares

and glam rock sex offenders.

Retro

held between brackets of jug and pot.

They'll only be used for ornament,

now.


These frozen chronotopes

form a row of boats

harboured from the storm

of austere cuts and glum faced news

beyond the pane.

They remember all too well

the black-outs, the unemployed

and the country doomed,

and so each handle catches

a smear of late afternoon sun.

# Farewell These Walls

Farewell these walls

that we never made home.

The turn of the century workers' cottage

that was owned by usury

and never owned by me,

left now

to the deathwatch beetles and the damp.


Before we met,

the bachelor pad was,

at best,

a hearth for the bosom of brotherhood;

the door open

to those that needed love.

At worst,

a stage

of red baked London clay

that saw the repeated performance

of a man drown

after bottle after bottle after bottle

of Jesus' blood.


All the could-have-beens

and reasons that they weren't.

The cracks that won't need to be papered over

anymore.

The cracks across the plaster

that was once new.


When we moved out

we cleaned and cleaned,

all memory expunged.

Sold now

to separate collateral

from damage,

the farewell's not fond

but several years overdue.

Perhaps, post partum,

there'll be a lament.

For now,

we're just glad to be shot of the place

and we close the soot streaked door

and walk away.

# The Word of

# Matthew

But now

these walls are

beyond every woken eye.


Beyond even Leary's

gaze that converts all those grand

mandates;

that covets and perpetuates

all four doors

that lead the watcher to the last

mode of chrome.


All four doors

open, and

the kraken of the marble,

the shardless truth,

narrowly recounts a fallacy.


As my pen gropes

all her nymphs would attend her

and every flavour counts;

through cosy clay morsels

that taste of almond or of cud.

# Gregor's Room

Free enough to scurry up the walls

and beyond,

as, next door, the full bearded lodgers

make themselves at home.

But that foul and lumpy scorn

of a sour faced charwoman

dumped the ashcan as a trophy of neglect

at the threshold

and from then on

the room became a junk heap.

The door stayed shut

and turn by turn,

gradually, she made a noun of refuse

and neglect of refuge.


Barely enough room to crawl,

freedom ceased, and melancholy returned

to feed the beast,

as even Grete could not bear

to look upon her brother

and be around such stench.

When they all could go on no more,

overcome by sleep,

he sought the end of honour.

He sought the darkest corner.

# Skeletons

These beams were once

part of a naval cutter or

a galleon bound for Florence

or for Naples

and now

she forms the frame

to dwell upon.

The notches that once held

pegs for map cases or

tools for tar or

the helmsman's eyeglass

are now

just spare mystery,

that looms over the lounge.

Anchored,

four thousand fathoms

from the shore,

the deep crust of sea salt

holds volumes of untold tales.

The Armada. The plumbed depths

of the slave trade.

She rarely speaks

but we long to hear the creak

as she crests the swell

from four hundred years past.

# The Plague Mask

From up there

your mortal end was a mere object,

one handed down a thousandfold.

To choose your end,

gloved and adorned,

you wear a mask of obdurate calm.

Lemon balm leaves, camphor and cloves

laudanum, myrrh and fresh petals of a rose,

storax, all can dull the stench

but not the eye.

You take frogs or leeches

from your doctor's bag

and put them on the buboes

to rebalance the humors

Your humourless beak

balanced on your nose.


Heal thyself;

whatsoever we have heard done, do here

but the part of you that's human seeps

from beneath the mask and,

though forlorn,

we smell your fear.

# Reverence

The poem

has an open mouth for every word

and a word for every mouth

that's closed.

The sounds

clack, eek, stumble,

prance and crack.

Each formed word leaps forth

full flow and then

cascades as one

shout,

one roar,

over the waterfall

to a well

of seamless sound.

Stop

and lend the sound your ear

as you've been asked before.

Hear the movement of more power

than words or mouths

alone

could ever muster.

Lower your head

to your reflected face

and slurp fulsomely.

Taste your story

amongst the words

of others.

The poem,

spoken aloud,

resounds.

# The Butcher of Madras

My father, the butcher of Madras,

became a surgeon of great renown.

Endless swarms of lepers queued for hours

and left as amputees.

From Tambaram and Andra Pradesh they came.

One wealthy raja from Bangalore

travelled seven days to lose a cursed thumb.

The reward for that successful severance

was gold.

England beckoned

to allow my father's seed a better set of chances

than the lepers and the amputees.

"Work hard," he would say.

"Work hard and you shall have your rewards."

He thought any of England's schools

were as good as Eton or St Pauls.

We worked hard at the bog-standard local comp,

turned our hands to our father's trade,

and learned to talk as well as any of our peers.


But where was he?

Tucked away, secreted, he butchered

on the conveyor belt of OAPs.

as he anonymously set replacement knees

for sedated elderly

whose loved ones then faltered when asked to care.

All the old renown was left unknown.

He was good though, and he looked good

on the Trust's charts and spreadsheets

but there were no rajas

and no gold.

Just the long slow fade

towards the grave.

# The Sexton and the Last

He took a job some summers past

(and everyone knew

that he wouldn't last), to care

for a sad church and the grounds round there;

to mend the patchwork of the roof and

take on the upkeep of the small haphazard graveyard.

Hopeful, he undertook

to make the deathly place a labour of love.


He planted hemlock; not

to everybody's taste.

He planted foxgloves

to keep hot hearts apace.

He weeded out speedwell

and knew, too well,

to leave the forget-me-nots

for those who wanted not

to be

forgot.


When all the day's work was complete

and often that was

before the church bell struck noon,

he would make the days replete

by book and page.

Under shaded boughs,

Marvell, Donne and the Bard

sated a hunger to be,

amongst all else, sage.


But of all the poetry that he read

There was one –

*The Rape of the Lock* –

that ran

untamed

through the trammels of the Sexton's head.

*To know such depth as Pope;*

*to see, as he, the sylphs,*

*the gnomes, nymphs*

*and salamanders.*

Others, less learned,

could not see them

and gave the sexton long stares

of reproach

as he would mumble verse

as they approached

for evensong.

The scolds spoke of Satan,

that he was possessed,

but the pastor,

(who adored poetry

as much as the Lord

and knew the sexton's heart)

spoke of love.

That was

up to the day

when love

took the pastor's words away.


...


Mary, the tanner's daughter,

the beauty of the maypole dance,

thought herself somewhat grand

and oft refused the farm boy's hand

for she had her eye

on wealth, or

on the brass buttons of a red coat, or

on the pure rugged power of a true man.

As she passed

by the gate, the sexton

stopped.

He leant upon the spade

that had also

stopped.

The very ground

he was meant to turn

had stopped.


Her locks, he saw, fell,

sausage curls to splendour,

and draped about her naked neck,

and he searched for the army of sylphs

around her head

that were surely there

to protect her aspect,

to blazon to the world

her wholesome worth

as a mortal goddess

of the earth.


Mary met the eye

of the lonesome sexton,

found her own well met, and,

aware of the pure rugged power

of a true man,

she announced,

"Men have fallen at my feet"

so


he fell.


...


They swore a tryst

between each mass

so that the flock would

not have need to feed on

rumours of young love.

For the tanner's daughter,

secrecy was paramount.

The vernal freshness of the land,

now that summer was close at hand,

brought forth the palette of May's blossoms.

The sexton found that he had

a roused heart                    and more.

As the verdant shoots of June

turned full leaf

to the heavens,

the sexton saw that she had

offered soft hope to savour         and more.

And when the long days evened

to the star pocked black,

the sexton dared to dream that he had

grace and favour

to taste the flavour of gentle caress and more.


Entranced, enraptured and entrapped,

the sexton's fall

for the tanner's daughter

was complete.


Often the work would go undone

as they

would slumber for shaded hours,

and he

would look upon her flaxen locks

and read her

poetry of great repute.


Between Pentecost and Lammas,

Mary assumed

she held the sexton's heart

and, as such, was well content.

Her goal, to love a man,

to be held and

be beholden,

had been

well met.

So,

under

a well waxed

moon

they

made

love.

Bladed,

they carved

each other's names.

The herald of Eros

scarred across beech bark;

two names surrounded by a heart

at the edge of the Sexton's graveyard,

an arrow through the lovers' mark.

...

But by the day of Holy Cross,

the tanner's daughter had bored of Pope,

she'd bored of Marvell, Donne and the Bard.

But of all the poetry that he read

There was one –

*The Rape of the Lock* –

that drove her from the sexton's bed.

She'd even begun to start to hope

that the sexton could be another man,

to dream he was a man of wealth

and power

that would buy her jewellery

and scour the earth

for treasure to show her worth,

and carry a watercolour of her

locket-bound

around the neck.

At harvest, her dreams

almost

came true.

She saw the pure rugged power

of a true man.

Her eyes poured over the hero of some

of her dreams;

they poured over the brass buttons

on the red coat he wore;

they poured over the sheathed sword

that hung close by two well toned legs;

they poured over the golden medal

on the man's broad and decorated chest.

Courage spoke volumes

and her courage spoke

and beckoned forth

the brave redcoat.

They had met just once and,

entranced, enraptured and entrapped,

she gave way,

and under the very next full moon

they made love.

For the tanner's daughter,

secrecy was paramount

but a red coat makes poor camouflage

and the sylphs,

the gnomes, nymphs

and salamanders

have eyes everywhere.


The sexton, who had heard

hushed tones

from the tongues of crones

who feed on

rumours of young love,

set out

to spy on treachery.

He was too late

to see that he was cuckold.

The redcoat had left

at dawn

and let the latch fall gently,

so as not to wake the tanner's daughter,

her flaxen locks a mess of lust

across her bed.

But the young man's leather boots

had marked a path

across the dew

and the gnomes and salamanders knew

to ward the sexton

of the course.

The nymphs sang;

the sound of fear

bubbled through the sexton's very core

and the salamanders drew up

and framed the cottage door.

He opened the latch and,

dewy eyed, she woke.


The sexton spoke.


She could only attempt,

to try and try,

to seek the ways to deny

the story of the scolds

but

the sylphs caught her words

and made her falter.

Her bare breasts, brazen to the deed,

dashed the sexton's hope.

The truth, though never told,

was clear.

She had bored of Pope.

He saw all at once the sylphs,

the gnomes, nymphs

and salamanders

dance through

a blackened charnel house

but he would not,

could not lay a hand on her

nor even let an eye to fall on her face.

All softness that he once saw,

all of the splendour,

was no more;

expunged from thought.

He turned and raced,

back to the shelter

of Marvell, Donne and the Bard.


Rage soaked, by All Hallows

he had composure just enough

to speak.

The pastor spoke of the Lord and of poetry

And so

the hot hand

of the sexton,

haunted by love,

took up a pen

and took a dagger of prosody

to the absent redcoat's throat.

So bladed, he wrote

verse

as dull and dreary

as any poem you could ever read.

Full stops went unused

because –

for an unkempt

and unfettered heart –

love flowed.


The rotten leaves fed

the gorged flowerbeds

around graves.

Word on word,

stanza on stanza,

such a wanton stream of verse

took a heavy toll.

There was no hope

to match the wonders

of Donne or Pope.

What he felt was too raw

even for the Bard.

He took a tack

and hammered the scroll

of verse to the great dark elm

that he'd always thought

was the graveyard's helm.

And, one late autumn afternoon,

the sexton dug around

an unmarked grave and –

alas – he came upon a skull.

The world he owned

had become a solemn necromunda.


He sloped, sorrow steeped,

to the elm and,

day by day,

scratched each letter

through the soggy parchment

of the scroll and on

to the elm's bark beneath.

There

the story of the sexton's fall

and the love

for the tanners daughter,

the very words

from the sexton's pen,

stay

embossed

upon the trunk

to the very day.

# Pax

The flowers and the candles

are here

to protect us.

# Other Patrician Press Titles

*Disarming the Porcupine* by Mark Brayley

Paperback 978-0-9927235-1-4 £7.50 and e-book edition

*The Unfettered Cube* by Mark Brayley

Paperback 978-0-9934945-1-2 £7.50 and e-book edition

*Four Quartets – T S Eliot and Spirituality* by Richard Brock

Paperback 978-0-99323-880-2 £7.95

*Arcobaleno Rainbow* by Sara Elena Rossetti

Paperback 978-0-9927235-5-2 £7.95 and e-book edition

*Three Wishes* by Philip Terry

Paperback 978-0-9927235-7-6 £5.00 and e-book edition

*Robert Macfarlane's Orphans* by Martin Johnson

Paperback 978-0-9932388-7-1 £7.50